PLAY and LEARN

with your 3 year old

56 simple activities

Learn while having fun

Quality time for parents and children

The activities in this book are organized into the following sections:

Special thanks to Joan Henry and Jean Tuemmler, my Mulberry Tree teaching team.

Congratulations on your purchase of some of the finest teaching materials in the world.

For information about other Evan-Moor products, call 1-800-777-4362 or FAX 1-800-777-4332

Visit our website http://www.evan-moor.com. Check the Product Updates link for supplements, additions, and corrections for this book.

Author: Jill Norris
Editor: Marilyn Evans
Copy Editor: Cathy Harber
Illustrator: Cindy Davis
Designer: Cheryl Puckett
Desktop: Carolina Caird
Cover: Cheryl Puckett

Entire contents ©1999 by EVAN-MOOR CORP.
18 Lower Ragsdale Drive, Monterey, CA 93940-5746.
Permission is hereby granted to the individual purchaser to reproduce student materials in this book for noncommercial individual or classroom use only. Permission is not granted for schoolwide, or systemwide, reproduction of materials.
Printed in U.S.A.

Evan-Moor
EDUCATIONAL PUBLISHERS

EMC 4502

How to Play and Learn with Your Three-Year-Old

What can I do to help my three-year-old learn and have fun at the same time? This book answers that question with 56 simple activities that parents can do as they spend quality time with their three-year-olds. Each activity is fun <u>and</u> provides a positive learning experience.

Play and learn at bath time or when you're waiting in line. Have activities ready if you're riding in the car and when your child is getting ready for bed. Sitting at the table, playing outside, or sharing a story—wherever you are and whatever you're doing—you can provide the kinds of experiences that build the foundation for future learning.

Use this book as a resource. Read over the activities to become familiar with them, but don't worry about doing them precisely. Enjoy the special time you spend with your child and remember:

- **Three-year-olds want to please.**

    Typical three-year-olds want to do things correctly. They are highly susceptible to praise and favorable comments. They also tend to be responsive to friendly humor.

- **Many three-year-olds have strong motor skills.**

    Three-year-olds are gaining command of their bodies. They walk well, run easily, and turn sharp corners. They are usually sure and agile.

- **Three-year-olds love new words.**

    In addition to their increased interest in books and storytelling, many three-year-olds love hearing new and different words. Introduce words and explain their meanings. Remember, the idea of a "surprise" or a "secret" is especially intriguing to most three-year-olds.

The intellectual and social stimulation that you provide as your child grows is important. Spend time with your three-year-old.
- Talk to your child.
- Play with your child.
- Read to your child.

Helping your child learn about the world is easy and fun!

Building Blocks to Learning

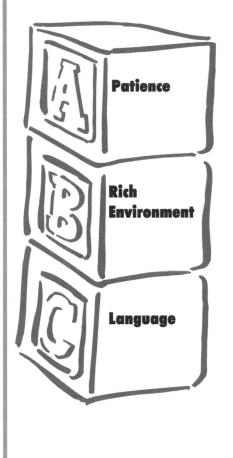

Three can be a conforming age. Some three-year-olds enjoy doing things with other children. However three-year-olds can also be stubborn. Be patient and stay out of conflict when you can.

It isn't necessary to buy expensive educational toys and materials in order to provide a rich environment for your child. Simple playthings like paint and clay help children develop creativity. Your three-year-old will give you clues about the kinds of experiences and play equipment that suits him or her. Listen to the questions asked and notice interest or lack of interest. Remember one of the most important things in your child's environment is you.

Three-year-olds confirm what they are doing with words. They ask for information, tell about their experiences, and call attention to their accomplishments. Reinforce their language use by talking and listening. Build on their awareness of the different sounds within words. Play with the sounds of language—make up silly words, create crazy rhymes, and whisper. This language play is an important step in prereading.

Skills for Success

Each page in *Play and Learn* is labeled to tell which skill areas are developed by the activity. Often a single activity addresses several different skills. You help to build the foundation for your child's success in school when you provide practice in these six important skills:

 Large-Motor Development
walking, running, jumping, large-muscle movement

 Coordination and Dexterity
small-muscle movements in the hands and fingers

 Language Development
speaking, listening, and developing vocabulary

 Creativity
imagining, exploring different materials, thinking in new ways

 Problem Solving
finding alternative solutions, understanding cause and effect

Memory and Concentration
remembering, connecting different ideas

Bath Time

Splash and chat
in the tub.
It's fun to learn
while I scrub.

Play and Learn to

- learn about the concepts empty and full
- develop vocabulary
- explore the properties of air and water
- make predictions and test them
- compare similar objects
- learn the best way to get clean

Activities

Which Holds the Most?

Fill one container with bath water and then pour it into another.

What You Need

- 3 plastic containers of different sizes and shapes

- bathtub and water

What You Do

1. Ask your child to pick one container and fill it with water.

2. Have your child pick a second container and fill it with water from the first container. Repeat this to fill the remaining container.

3. Ask questions to encourage comparisons. Point to the containers as you ask,

    Did this one hold more water than that one?
    How can you tell?
    Which one holds the most?

4. After exploring all three containers, help your child arrange them in order by the amount that they hold.

Point to the cup your child thought held the most and put it on the edge of the bathtub. Look at the other two containers. Ask,

Which held the most?

Place the container next in line. Put the last container at the end of the line.

The Parts of My Body

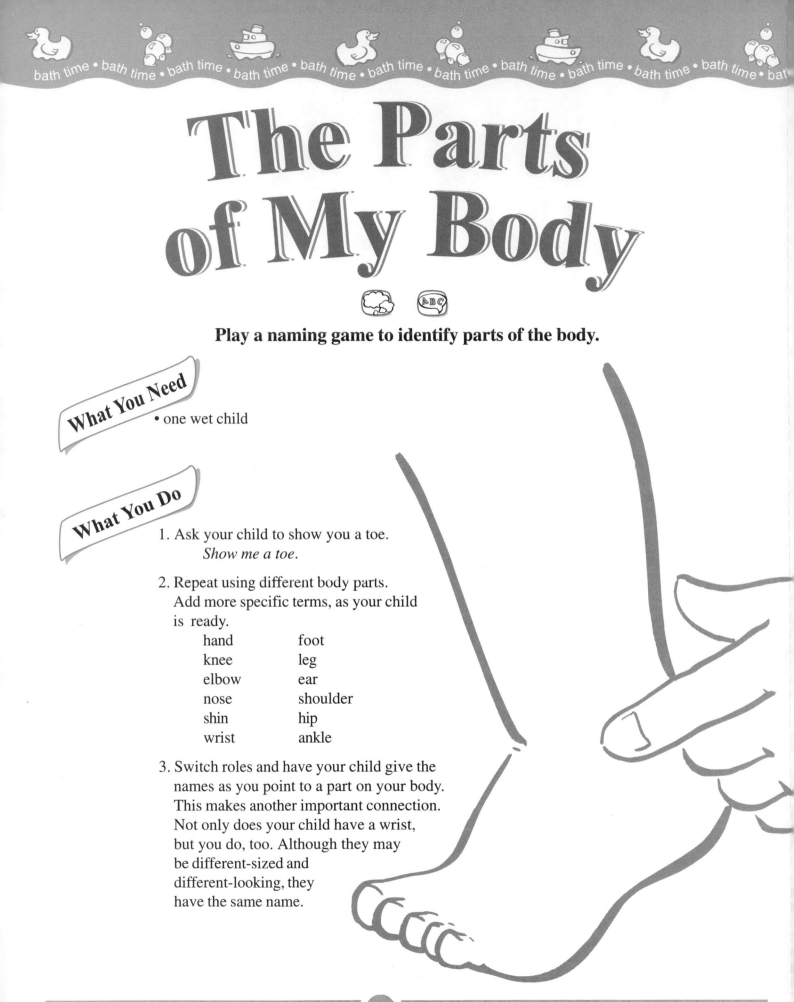

Play a naming game to identify parts of the body.

What You Need

• one wet child

What You Do

1. Ask your child to show you a toe.
   Show me a toe.

2. Repeat using different body parts. Add more specific terms, as your child is ready.

hand	foot
knee	leg
elbow	ear
nose	shoulder
shin	hip
wrist	ankle

3. Switch roles and have your child give the names as you point to a part on your body. This makes another important connection. Not only does your child have a wrist, but you do, too. Although they may be different-sized and different-looking, they have the same name.

Bubbles, Bubbles, Bubbles

Blowing bubbles in the bath is a blast!

What You Need

• a bubble wand

• jar of bubble solution or make your own

Caution: Keep bubble solution out of your child's eyes.

What You Need

1. Dip the wand in the bubble solution.

2. Hold the solution-coated wand in front of your mouth.

3. Blow toward the hole in the wand.

4. After you and your child enjoy blowing the bubbles, try
   • counting the bubbles
   • clapping the bubbles
   • catching the bubbles on the wand without popping them

5. Talk about what causes the bubbles and why they move the way they do. Put ideas in kid-language.

Bubble Solution

Ingredients:
   ¼ cup (50 ml) of dishwashing liquid
   ¾ cup (175 ml) of cold water
   5 drops of glycerin (You can buy glycerin at a pharmacy.)
Mix all ingredients together.
Store the bubble solution in a covered container.

Will It Float? Will It Sink?

Float and sink familiar bathroom objects.

What You Need

- bathroom objects—soap, washcloth, rubber duck, comb, toothpaste tube, plastic cup, bath toys

- tub of water

What You Do

1. Drop an object into the water. Ask your child to describe what happened.
   What happened to the soap when I dropped it into the water?
   Did it sink? Did it float?
   If your child is not familiar with the terms *sink* and *float,* show what the words mean by floating something and sinking something.

2. Show your child another object. Have your child predict whether the object will sink or float. Then have your child test the prediction.

3. Continue with a variety of objects. Always predict, test, and then sort into two piles—**Sink** and **Float**!

Add objects from other rooms in the house or do the activity outdoors with a washtub of water.

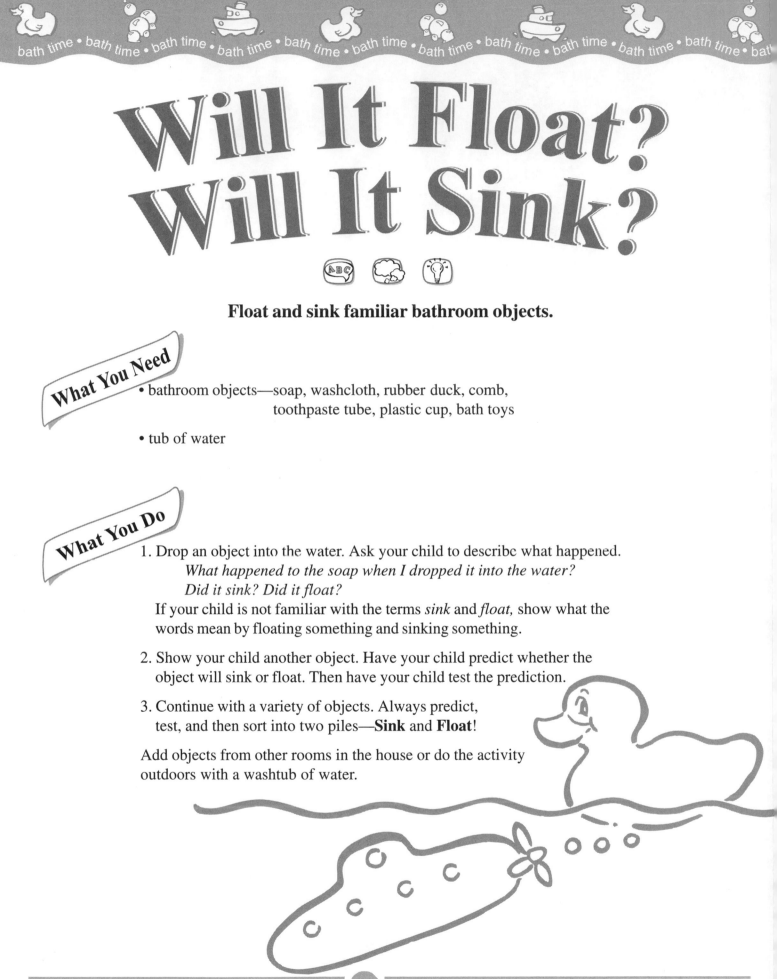

Sink the Boat

How much will a toy boat hold before it sinks?

What You Need

- toy boat
- tub of water
- supply of pennies

What You Do

1. Float the toy boat in the tub.

2. Ask your child to predict how many pennies the boat will hold before it sinks.

3. Have your child add one penny at a time to the boat. Count the pennies as they are added.

4. Continue until the boat sinks.

5. Check the prediction.

Try the same activity with a bigger boat and a smaller boat.

Change It and Watch

Make a plastic cup sink or float by making changes.

What You Need

- a plastic cup
- a tub of water

What You Do

Encourage your child to explore the sinking and floating of a plastic cup as changes are made to the cup.

What happens when you put the cup in the water?
Will the same thing happen if the cup is upside down?
Will the same thing happen if the cup is on its side?
What happens if the cup is half full of water?
What happens if the cup is full of water?
What other changes can you make?
Will it sink or float now?

What's the Best Way?

When your three-year-old comes in really dirty, take the opportunity to learn about how to get really clean.

What You Need

- washcloth
- bar of soap
- tub of water

What You Do

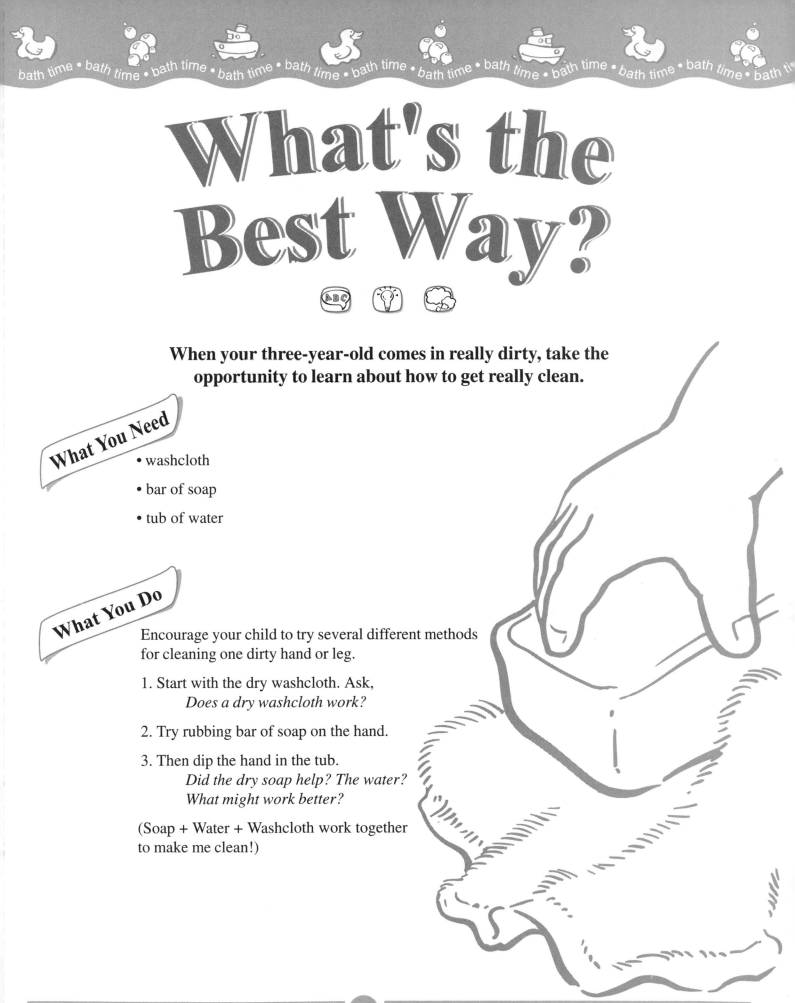

Encourage your child to try several different methods for cleaning one dirty hand or leg.

1. Start with the dry washcloth. Ask,
   Does a dry washcloth work?

2. Try rubbing bar of soap on the hand.

3. Then dip the hand in the tub.
   Did the dry soap help? The water?
   What might work better?

(Soap + Water + Washcloth work together to make me clean!)

How Fast Will It Dry?

Discover the fastest way to dry something.

What You Need

• 4 washcloths

What You Do

1. Put the 4 washcloths in the bathtub to get them uniformly wet.

2. Decide on an area where the washcloths can be left until they dry.

3. Spread one washcloth out flat to dry.
   Wad up one washcloth and leave it wadded up to dry.
   Wring out one washcloth and spread it out flat to dry.
   Wring out one washcloth, wad it up, and leave it to dry.

4. Predict which will dry first. Wait and watch as the cloths dry. Check them often. Ask,
   Which washcloths dried first?
   Which was the slowest?
   How will what we learned help us?

5. Try the same activity leaving one wet washcloth in the sun and one in a shaded area.

Bathtub Paint

Create a masterpiece on the side of the tub and then rinse it away.

What You Need

• bathtub paint (Purchase tubes at a toy store or make your own.)

• bathtub

What You Do

1. Squeeze or spoon a small dollop of paint onto the artist's hand.

2. Encourage the artist to use a finger or hand to draw.

At first, this drawing will probably be simply smearing color on an area of the tub. Encourage your child to experiment with textures and different techniques. Suggest some changes by showing new techniques. Praise creative work.

• Change and mix the colors.
• Use a finger to wipe off the color to make a picture or write a name.
• Try making the paint smooth and then bumpy.

Bathtub Paint

Ingredients:
    1 cup (200 g) of soap flakes
    2 tablespoons (30 ml) of water + food coloring

1. Mix detergent with colored water.
2. Beat with egg beater until smooth.
3. Store in a covered container.

Mealtime

I'm the cook's assistant.
I do important tasks.
I wash and wrap and scrub.
I do whatever he asks.
I'm the cook's assistant.
I butter and I beat.
I pour and shake and stir.
And then, of course, I eat!

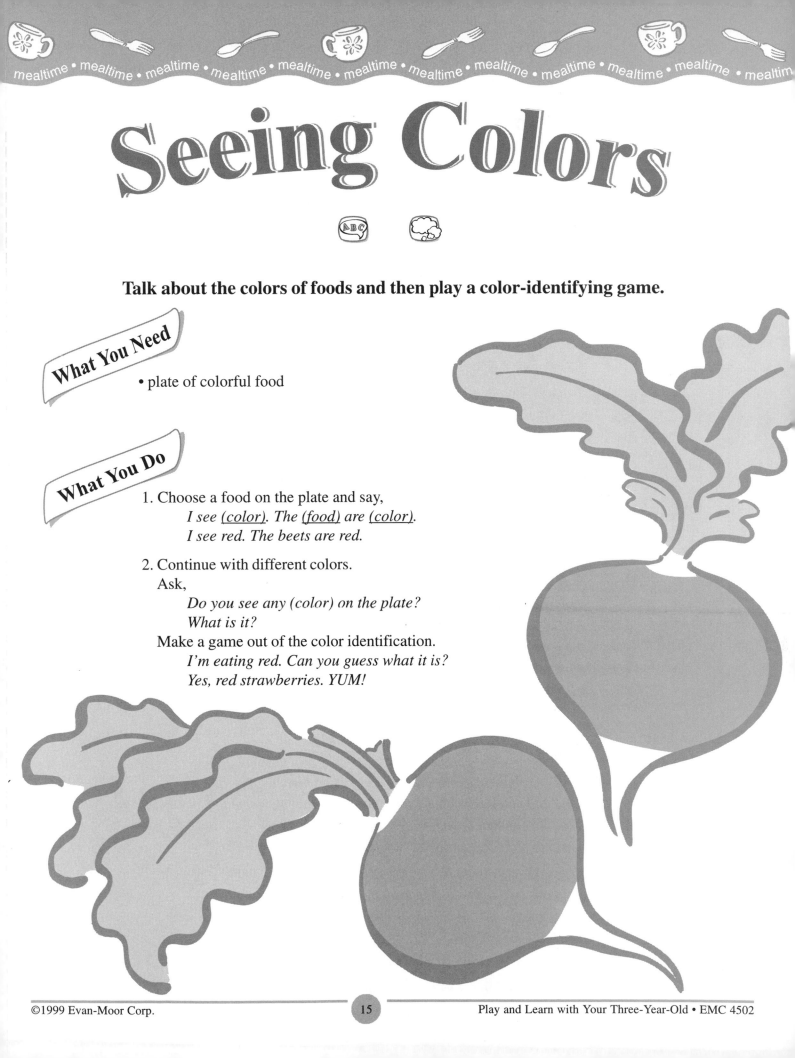

Seeing Colors

Talk about the colors of foods and then play a color-identifying game.

What You Need

• plate of colorful food

What You Do

1. Choose a food on the plate and say,
   I see (color). The (food) are (color).
   I see red. The beets are red.

2. Continue with different colors.
   Ask,
   Do you see any (color) on the plate?
   What is it?
   Make a game out of the color identification.
   I'm eating red. Can you guess what it is?
   Yes, red strawberries. YUM!

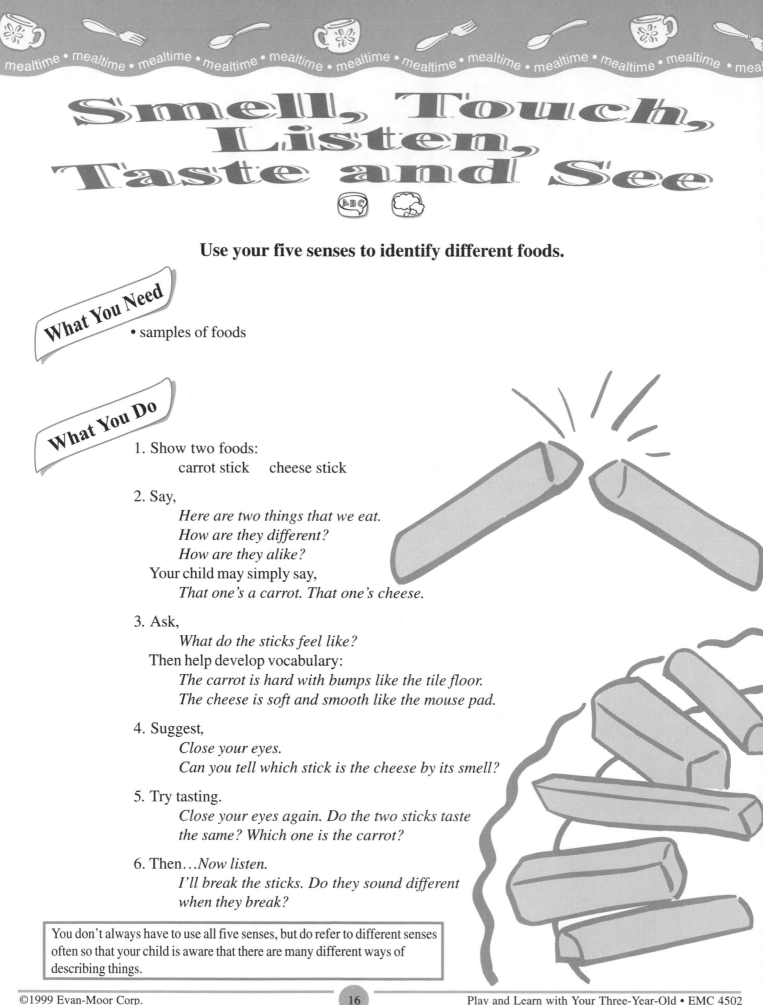

Smell, Touch, Listen, Taste and See

Use your five senses to identify different foods.

What You Need

• samples of foods

What You Do

1. Show two foods:
   carrot stick   cheese stick

2. Say,
   Here are two things that we eat.
   How are they different?
   How are they alike?
   Your child may simply say,
   That one's a carrot. That one's cheese.

3. Ask,
   What do the sticks feel like?
   Then help develop vocabulary:
   The carrot is hard with bumps like the tile floor.
   The cheese is soft and smooth like the mouse pad.

4. Suggest,
   Close your eyes.
   Can you tell which stick is the cheese by its smell?

5. Try tasting.
   Close your eyes again. Do the two sticks taste the same? Which one is the carrot?

6. Then…*Now listen.*
   I'll break the sticks. Do they sound different when they break?

You don't always have to use all five senses, but do refer to different senses often so that your child is aware that there are many different ways of describing things.

It's a Pattern!

Engage the help of your three-year-old in putting out the silverware or napkins for a meal.

What You Need

- silverware
- napkins
- small basket

What You Do

1. Count the silverware that you will use and place it in a small basket. Count aloud and describe what you are doing.

   Four of us will be eating lunch today, so we will need four spoons, four forks, four knives, and four napkins.
   1–2–3–4 spoons
   1–2–3–4 forks
   1–2–3–4 knives
   1–2–3–4 napkins

2. Have your child carry the basket to the table.

3. As you put out a plate, your child puts a napkin on the plate.

4. Together you put forks, spoons, and knives by the plates.

Soon your child will be able to put out the spoons, forks, knives, and napkins without help. Be sure to thank your child for the help.

The Shape of Things

Prepare a meal by making food shapes and then enjoy eating circles or squares.

What You Need

• foods cut into circles or squares

Sample Circle Menu
- Carrot coins
- Cracker stacks (round crackers layered with cheese)
- Banana slices
- Salami

Sample Square Menu
- French Toast (trim bread into squares before cooking)
- Pat of butter
- Melon cubes

What You Do

1. Sit down at the table with your child. Introduce the "shape of the day."
   The slice of salami is a circle shape.
   Do you see any other circles?

2. Eat. Point out and enjoy the circles on the plate. As you are eating, you may want to look around for other objects in the room that are circles too.
   The clock on the wall is a circle.

3. Another day enjoy a meal of square shapes. When your child seems comfortable with circle and square shapes, serve a meal using two shapes and practice identifying the two shapes as you eat.

I Can Help

Your three-year-old learns by imitating your everyday kitchen routine.

What You Need

• low cupboard or drawer

• an accessible work surface

• plastic measuring cups, plastic or wooden spoons, a plastic bowl, small saucepan, dish towel, spatula, any other kitchen utensils that are safe to use

• a small scrubbing pad or brush

Note: Use a plastic picnic knife or a table knife. Don't expect your child to cut anything that requires a sharp knife.

What You Do

1. Designate an area for storing your three-year-old's kitchen equipment. This area should be accessible so that your child can use the equipment to:
   • imitate your work in the kitchen
   • explore stirring, pouring, spreading, and measuring
   • help prepare food for meals

2. Some specific jobs your three-year-old can do include:
   scrubbing—potatoes, carrots
   tearing—lettuce, parsley, basil
   breaking—cauliflower, broccoli, asparagus
   shelling—peas, beans
   stirring—batter, yogurt, egg salad
   cutting—eggs, cheese, bananas, melon
   wrapping—hot dogs in dough, potatoes in foil
   rolling—dough
   shaking—pudding, chocolate milk

Cook with Me!

The following four picture recipes are for single-portion snacks that my children loved when they were three years old. At first, work side by side with your child to prepare the snacks. Later, your child will be able to prepare his or her own snack independently.

Magic Pudding

Ingredients:

    1 cup (240 ml) of milk
    2 tablespoons (28 g) of instant pudding mix

Combine milk and pudding mix in a small covered container. Make sure cover is securely in place, and shake for several minutes.

Lemonade

Ingredients:

    ½ lemon
    ice cubes
    2 teaspoons (8 g) of sugar
    ⅓ cup (80 ml) of water

Combine the ingredients in a glass. Stir and add ice cubes.

Fruit Salad

Ingredients:

½ of a banana
1 slice of pineapple
6 seedless grapes
small slice of melon without rind

Put the fruit in a small bowl.
Stir and eat.

Sandwich Surprise

Ingredients:

round slice of baguette
slice of Canadian bacon
grated Swiss cheese

Layer the bacon and cheese on the bread. Melt cheese in a microwave.

Pretzel Stick Counter

This simple snack helps develop small-motor coordination while you practice counting.

What You Need

- pretzel sticks
- dollop of peanut butter or a cube of fairly soft cheese
- Cheerios®

What You Do

1. Stand the pretzel upright in the dollop of peanut butter or the cube of cheese.

2. Have your child put Cheerios®, one by one, on the pretzel pole.

3. Count the Cheerios® on the pole.

Use several pretzel poles and compare the number of Cheerios® on the poles to help your child understand the concept of more and less.
This pole has more Cheerios® than that pole.

Cherry Cubes

Making cherry ice cubes not only helps your child practice one-to-one correspondence, but also helps to show how water can change from liquid to solid and back again.

What You Need

- water
- cherries or grapes
- ice cube tray

What You Do

1. Have your child put one cherry in each section of an ice cube tray. Describe what is happening.

   You put one cherry in each hole.
   There are 12 holes.
   1–2–3–4–5–6–7–8–9–10–11–12
   There are 12 cherries.
   1–2–3–4–5–6–7–8–9–10–11–12

2. Using a small pitcher, your child fills the tray with water.

3. Put the tray in the freezer for several hours. Help your child to remove the cubes from the tray. Talk about how the water changed.

   Remember how you poured the water into the tray with the pitcher? Does the water pour now? How is it different?

Use the cherry cubes in lemonade or sparkling water for a special treat.

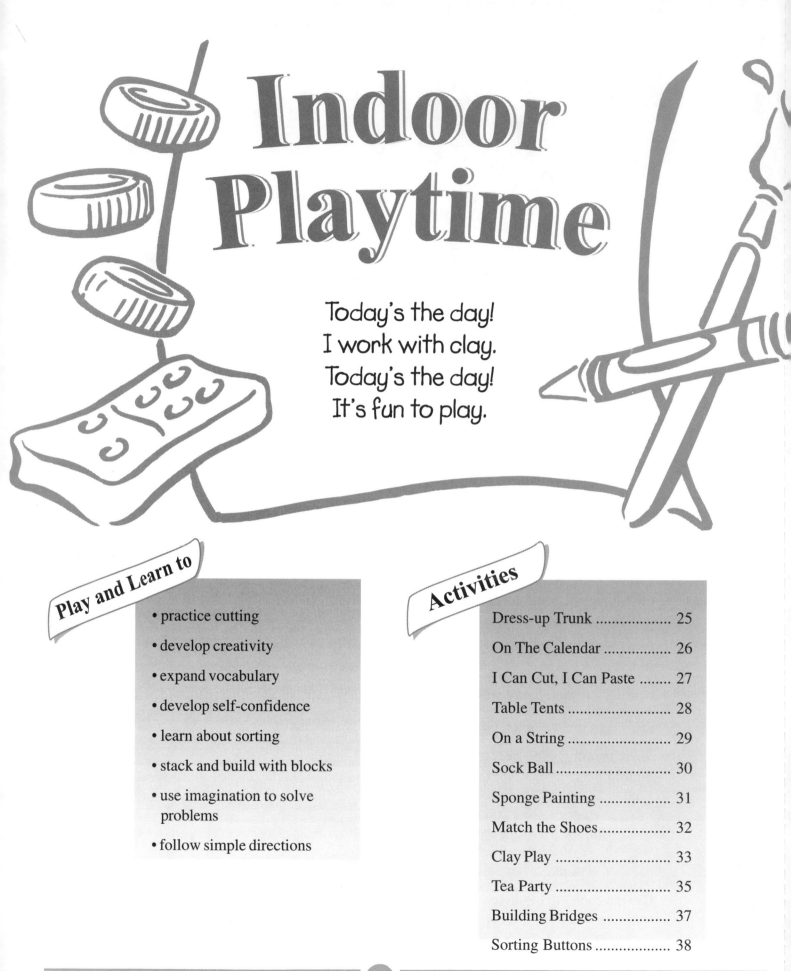

Indoor Playtime

Today's the day!
I work with clay.
Today's the day!
It's fun to play.

Play and Learn to

- practice cutting
- develop creativity
- expand vocabulary
- develop self-confidence
- learn about sorting
- stack and build with blocks
- use imagination to solve problems
- follow simple directions

Activities

Dress-up Trunk

Since three-year-olds love to imitate grown-ups and imagine themselves in grown-up situations, collect a few props to store in a special box or trunk.

What You Need

- box or trunk

- several hats, shawls, vest, etc.

What You Do

1. Store the clothing items in the trunk. Put the trunk in a place that is accessible to your child. (Whenever you clean your closet, add a few new items to the trunk.)

2. Join your child in imaginary play. Put on a hat and adopt a new persona. Let your child direct the play.

    Daddy goes to work. Don't forget your lunch, Daddy.

On the Calendar

Help your three-year-old to *see* time by using a large calendar to mark off the days.

What You Need

• large calendar with space by each day to write or draw

What You Do

1. Post the calendar in a highly visible spot, such as the door of your child's room or the refrigerator.

2. Mark important days that are upcoming. Draw small pictures to represent what you did on specific days.

3. Each day, have your child circle the current day and cross off the previous day.

4. Encourage your three-year-old to suggest things to record on the calendar.
   Today we're going to the park.
   Let's draw a slide on the calendar.

I Can Cut, I Can Paste

Help your child to learn the basic skills necessary to cut and paste to make an abstract collage.

What You Need

- small pieces of colored paper (wrapping paper, Sunday funnies, magazine pages, or any paper that cuts easily)

- child scissors (Try the scissors to make sure that they cut before you buy them. If your child is left-handed, try them left-handed.)

- larger piece of construction paper

- paste

> Don't expect the cut-paper collage to be a picture of something. Just enjoy the colors and shapes.

What You Do

1. Show your child how to hold the scissors.
   - Hold the scissors with the thumb on top and the pointer finger underneath.
   - Gently support your child's hand at first to help keep the scissors' blades perpendicular to the paper.
   - Move the thumb and the pointer finger to open and close the scissors' blades.

2. Have your child cut the colored papers into pieces.

3. Put a glob of paste on a small paper plate and show your child how to paste.
   - Rub one finger on the paste.
   - Rub the paste on the back of the paper.
   - Put the paper paste-side down on the construction paper.

4. Continue to paste the pieces to the large piece of construction paper.

Table Tents

A folding table and a sheet become a special place for make-believe.

What You Need

- folding table
- flat sheet

What You Do

1. Put up two legs of the table to form the frame for the tent.

2. Cover the frame with a sheet.

3. Furnish the tent with several small pillows and books. A flashlight makes an especially fun addition.

4. Join your child for a read-aloud time in the tent.

To accommodate a larger crowd in the tent, extend all four table legs.

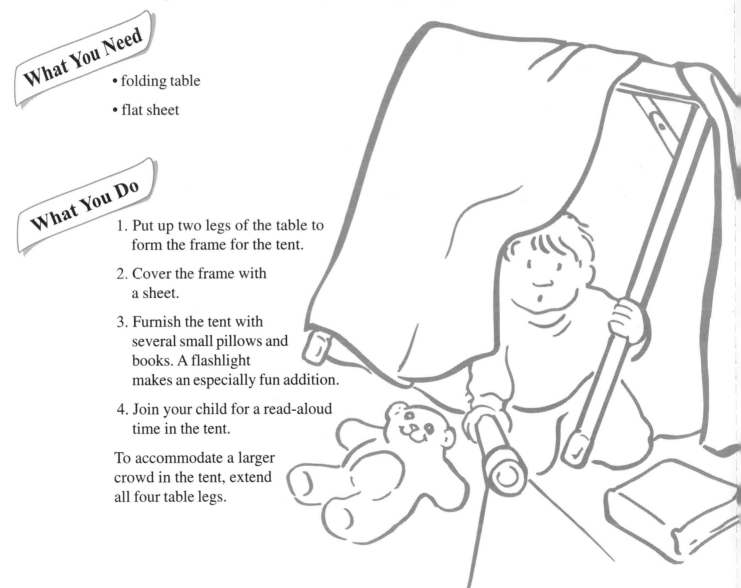

On a String

String large beads on a shoelace and then hang them nearby to admire.

What You Need
- a wide shoestring
- large wooden beads

What You Do

1. Tie one bead to the end of the shoestring to act as the knot.

2. Show your child how to hold a bead with one hand and push the shoestring through the hole with the other hand.

3. When several beads are on the string, hang it from a hook and admire the beads.

4. Name the beads or count them.
   Red bead, red bead, blue bead.
   One bead, two beads, three beads—1, 2, 3

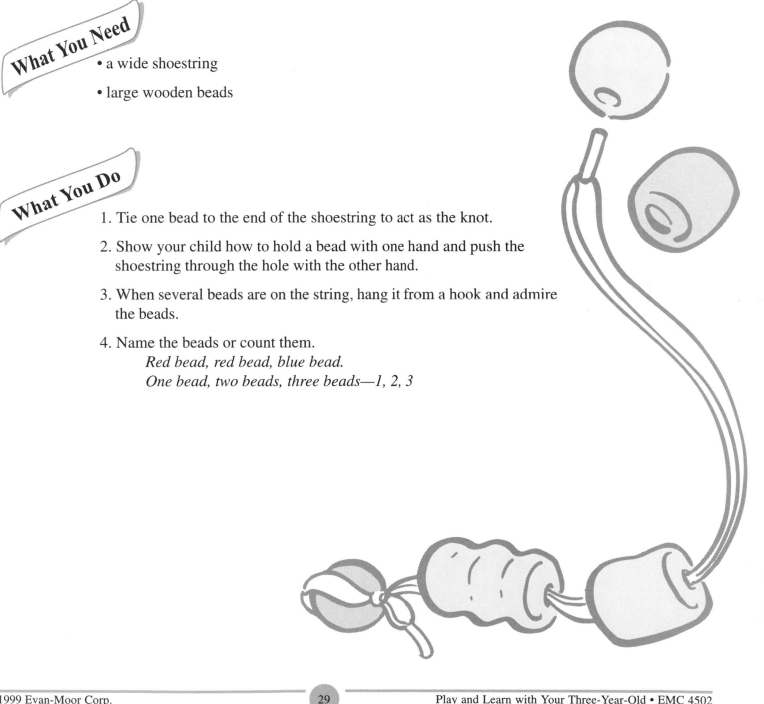

Sock Ball

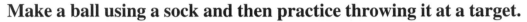

Make a ball using a sock and then practice throwing it at a target.

What You Need

- socks
- several small boxes

What You Do

1. Starting with the toe, roll each sock up and slip the cuff over the roll to form balls. Make several sock balls.

2. Make a target using the small boxes.
   - Place the boxes in a line about three feet from your child.
   - Tip the boxes toward your child by placing a book under the back edges.

3. Throw the sock balls. Try to get them into the boxes.

Sock balls are great for throwing and catching as well as target play.

Sponge Painting

**Use sponge prints to decorate brown paper bags.
Then use the bags for lunch sacks or gift wrap.**

What You Need

- small brown paper grocery bags
- sponges
- small tray
- tempera paint
- newspapers or plastic drop cloth

What You Do

1. Cover the area where you will be working with newspapers or a plastic drop cloth.

2. Pour a puddle of paint into the tray.

3. Dip the sponge into the paint.

4. Press the sponge onto the brown paper sack to make a sponge print.

5. Repeat dipping and printing.

You can also cut the sponge into different shapes or buy ready-made sponge shapes for your sponge prints.

Match the Shoes

Help your child to make pairs from a pile of mismatched shoes.

What You Need

• several pairs of shoes

Begin with one pair of your shoes and one pair of your child's shoes. Add more pairs (including pairs that are more similar) as your child gains expertise.

What You Do

1. Spread the shoes out on the floor.

2. Hold up one shoe. Have your child find its mate.

3. Repeat until all pairs are matched.

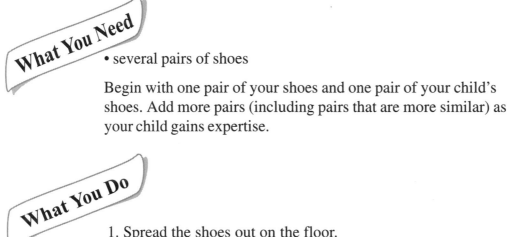

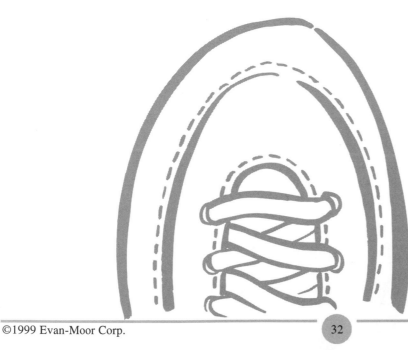

Clay Play

Explore the feel of different clays as you develop new vocabulary.

What You Need

• clay (purchased at the store or from homemade recipes on page 34)

• clean surface for shaping and rolling

What You Do

1. Simply enjoy making different shapes.
   Explore to see what works.

2. Talk about what you are doing as you do it.
   Use words that describe the actions and talk about
   how the clay feels.
   • Roll the dough into a ball.
     When I roll the dough it feels smooth.
   • Flatten the dough with your hand.
     I like to smash the dough flat with the palm of my hand.
   • Pinch the dough to make bumps.
     When I pinch the dough it makes little bumps.
   • Roll a long "snake."
     If I stretch and roll the dough I can make a snake. The snake is wiggly when I hold it up.
   • Coil the "snake" into circles.
     I wrap the snake around and around.
     This is called a coil.

Here are two recipes for dough I used when my children were three.

Baker's Clay

Ingredients:
- 1 cup (288 g) of salt
- 1½ cups (360 ml) of hot water
- 4 cups (500 g) of flour

1. Dissolve salt in hot water.

2. Stir in flour.

3. Knead until pliable (at least 5 minutes).

4. Store in an airtight container.

After shaping, bake at 250º F (120º C) until hard.
(The length of time will depend on the size and thickness of the object.)
When cool, color with markers, spray with clear acrylic glaze, and enjoy.

Recipe for Texture Dough

Ingredients:
- 2 cups (470 ml) of water
- ½ cup (144 g) of salt
- food coloring
- 2 tablespoons (30 ml) of salad oil
- 2 tablespoons (18 g) of alum
- 2 cups (250 g) of flour

1. Boil water, salt, and food coloring in a pan.

2. Remove from heat.

3. Add oil, alum, and flour.

4. While hot, mix and knead for five minutes.

5. Store in an airtight container.

This dough is called "texture dough" because you can knead in different ingredients to change the texture. Try adding sand, coffee grounds, sawdust, or glitter.

Note about ready-made clays: Oil-based clays leave oily marks on surfaces that can be difficult to clean. Playdough® is easy to shape and clean up, but it dries out quickly when exposed to the air.

indoor playtime • indoor playtime • indoor playtime • indoor playtime • indoor playtime • indoor playtime • indoor playtime • indoor playtin

Tea Party

Three-year-olds love tea parties. Share the party with a favorite stuffed animal or a friend.

What You Need

- cups and saucers
  (Small ones are great fun, but regular ones will do.)

- small pitcher or teapot

- herbal tea or juice (optional)

- cookies or tiny sandwiches (optional)

What You Do

1. Set a low table with the cups and saucers. (I used the base of my footstool without the cushion.)

2. Invite your child to join you for a special tea party.

3. Be rather formal as you sit down and pour the tea. (If you choose to use *pretend tea* you will have to *pretend pour*.)

4. Sip your tea and talk about the day's activities.

5. Repeat a tea party rhyme and sing *I'm a Little Teapot* (see page 36).

One of my friends spent a wonderful afternoon with her three-year-old. She and her daughter dressed in their best dresses. My friend actually wore a formal gown and white gloves. They sipped honey-sweetened tea and shared the occasion with a stuffed bunny wearing a velvet bow.

Here are two special tea party verses.
Enjoy them at your next tea party.

Here's a Cup

Here's a cup,
And here's a cup,
And here's a pot of tea.

Pour a cup,
And pour a cup,
And have a drink with me.

I'm a Little Teapot

I'm a little teapot,
Short and stout.
Here is my handle,
Here is my spout.
When I get all steamed up,
Hear me shout,
"Tip me over and pour me out."

Building Bridges

It's fun to "drive" a toy car across a bridge that you have built.

What You Need

- set of blocks—You can purchase a set of wooden or plastic blocks, or make your own from milk cartons.

- several flat pieces of cardboard in various sizes

How to Make Milk Carton Blocks

1. Wash empty half-gallon milk cartons.

2. Open the lips and tear open the top flaps.

3. Tape the ends flat with clear tape.

4. Cover the milk carton blocks with contact paper. (optional)

What You Do

1. Sit on the floor with your child.

2. Stack several blocks on top of each other to make one bridge tower. Build another bridge tower about two feet away from the first.

3. Use the cardboard pieces or long blocks to form ramps going up the towers and to form the actual span of the bridge.

4. "Drive" a toy car across the bridge.

Extend the activity by:
- designing more complicated bridges.
- connecting several bridges with ramps.
- making a child-size bridge using boxes and boards.

Sorting Buttons

Challenge your child to sort buttons into two groups.

What You Need

• a bowl of buttons (include different button sizes and shapes)

What You Do

1. Explain that you want to sort the buttons into two piles—the big buttons and the little buttons.

2. Work together to sort the buttons.

3. Change the categories and sort again.
   ### Sample Button Categories
Two-hole	Four-hole
Colored	White
Round	Other shapes

I still have Grandma's blue button bag. It is filled with buttons of every shape and size. My brothers and I sorted and counted them as children, my three children sorted them, and now my grandchildren love looking at them and choosing their favorites.

Outdoor Playtime

Dig and slide.
Climb and ride.
Run and hide.
It's fun outside.

Play and Learn to

- run, jump, hop, skip, and climb
- develop large-motor skills
- throw, catch, kick, and bounce balls
- improve coordination
- understand words like back, over, from, up, on top of, and underneath
- identify sources of sounds

Activities

Playground Play Group

Take advantage of your child's interest in other children to encourage cooperative play.

What You Need

• a neighborhood playground

What You Do

1. Invite one or two other parents of three-year-olds to join a playground play group.

2. Decide on a regular time to meet. Depending on your schedule, you may choose to meet every week or every month.

3. Meet at the playground to enjoy some time together.

Hints:
• Don't expect children to automatically play together. They will probably begin with parallel play and mature into group play.
• Keep expectations flexible and unregimented.
• Supervise the play and join in when appropriate.
• Visit new playgrounds occasionally and, for a special treat, go to a zoo or museum.

My daughter's play group met every week for two years. The group began with her three-year-old birthday party. We invited two of Amy's friends and their moms to the local playground. Party favors included sand pails and shovels. Amy is now 23 and I'm still in touch with the parents of her playmates.

Water Painting

"Paint" walls, trees, fences, gates, mailboxes, and lawn furniture with water.

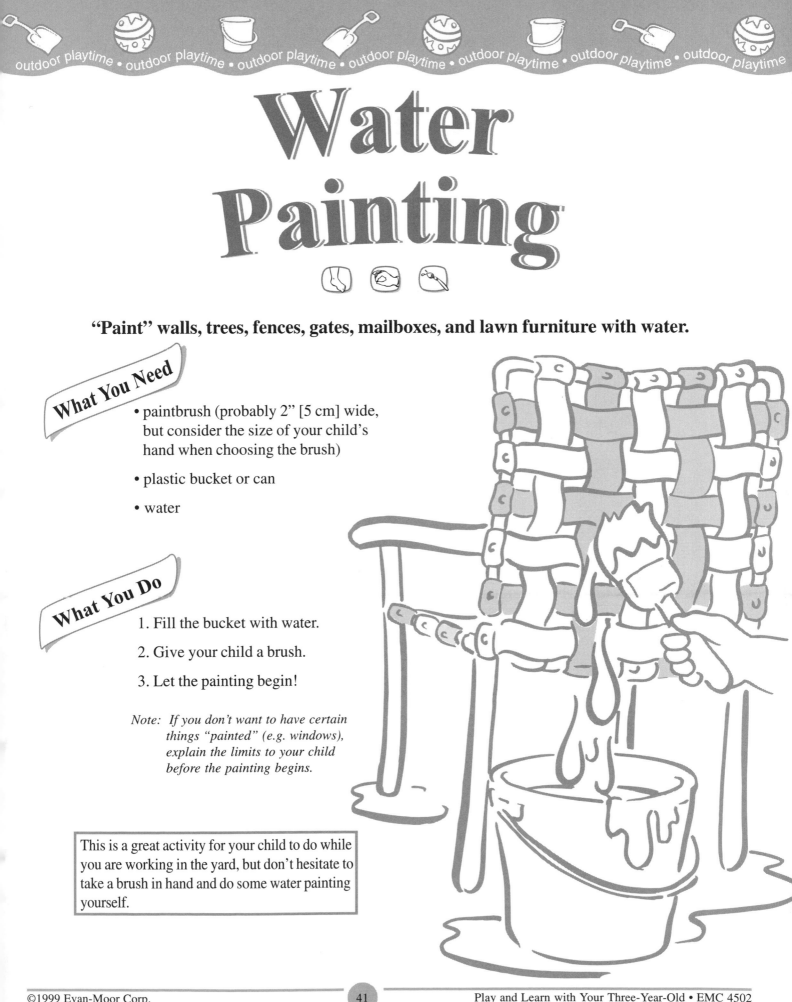

What You Need

- paintbrush (probably 2" [5 cm] wide, but consider the size of your child's hand when choosing the brush)

- plastic bucket or can

- water

What You Do

1. Fill the bucket with water.

2. Give your child a brush.

3. Let the painting begin!

Note: If you don't want to have certain things "painted" (e.g. windows), explain the limits to your child before the painting begins.

This is a great activity for your child to do while you are working in the yard, but don't hesitate to take a brush in hand and do some water painting yourself.

Hop and Jump

Share your three-year-old's enthusiasm for mastering large-motor skills.

What You Need

• space for hopping and jumping

What You Do

1. Make sure that your child understands the difference between the two terms—*hop* and *jump*. If necessary, show your child how to balance on one foot and hop.

2. Play a game of jumping and hopping. Say,
   Hop 3 times. Jump 2 times.

3. Gradually make directions more complicated.
   Hop over to me.

4. Switch places with your child. You do the hopping and jumping.

Cement Artist

Your cement artist will enjoy drawing on the sidewalk or the driveway.

• playground chalk

• cement surface

1. Make the playground chalk with your child. The grinding and mixing is a great shared activity.

2. Use the chalk you created to draw beautiful pictures. Be sure to sign the drawings with your name.

Playground Chalk

Ingredients:
    12 eggshells
    2 tablespoons (18 g) of flour
    2 teaspoons (10 ml) of hot water
    paper towel

1. Wash and dry the eggshells.

2. Grind the eggshells to a fine powder with a rock.

3. Put the powder in a dish, discarding big pieces of shell.

4. Combine flour and hot water in a second dish.

5. Add crushed eggshell and mix until it sticks together.

6. Shape the mixture into a fat chalk-stick shape.

7. Roll tightly in paper towel and dry until it hardens.

Mud Pies

Practice measuring and mixing with dirt and water.

What You Need

- pail of "clean" dirt
- water
- plastic bowl, plate, spoon, cup

What You Do

1. Set up a low table or bench with the mud pie supplies.

2. Encourage your child to mix dirt and water to make mud that can be formed into shapes or poured into small pans.

3. Allow mud creations to dry in the sun.

4. Decorate with grass seeds and twigs.

Don't worry if your child simply enjoys the process of making mud. It isn't important that you end up with mud pies. The process is the important part. Your child is exploring liquids and solids and discovering how they change when they are combined.

Obstacle Course

Set up an obstacle course for your three-year-old tricycle rider.

What You Need

- several big cardboard boxes
- tricycle
- level area for riding

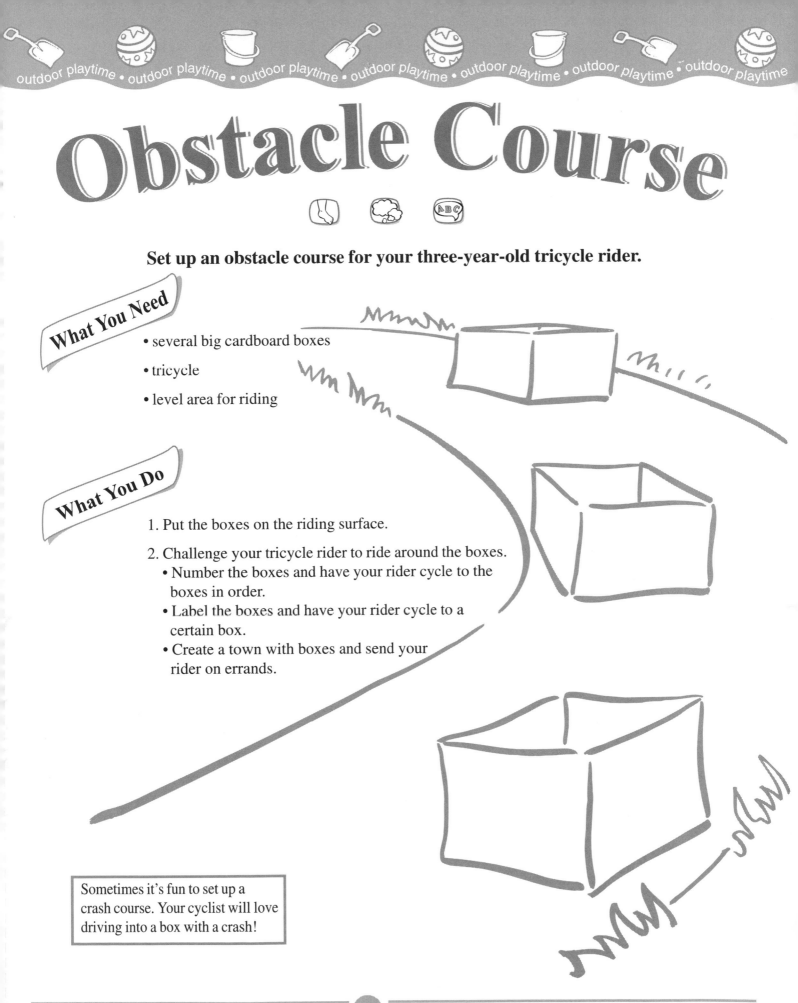

What You Do

1. Put the boxes on the riding surface.

2. Challenge your tricycle rider to ride around the boxes.
   - Number the boxes and have your rider cycle to the boxes in order.
   - Label the boxes and have your rider cycle to a certain box.
   - Create a town with boxes and send your rider on errands.

Sometimes it's fun to set up a crash course. Your cyclist will love driving into a box with a crash!

Walk-around Collage

Walk around your neighborhood gathering bits of bark, leaves, and other treasures. Then mount the treasures on a poster.

What You Need

- place to walk
- basket or bag
- piece of posterboard
- backpack with snack and water bottle (optional)

What You Do

1. Put on comfortable shoes, stick a snack in your backpack or bag, and fill your water bottle.

2. Walk with your child. Collect leaves, twigs, petals, and stones in your basket.

3. Talk about the things you see and the things that you put in your basket.

4. Glue or tape the "treasures" to a piece of posterboard. Add a date to the collage and a caption that tells where you walked.

Take the same walk during a different season and make another collage. Ask,

> *Are the things we saw the same?*
> *Do our collages look different?*

Raking Leaves

A child-size rake makes working alongside a parent fun.

What You Need

- small rake and a big rake
- basket
- leaves

What You Do

1. Go outside with your child.

2. Show your child how to use a rake to pile up the leaves.

3. Work together to clear an area and make a small pile of leaves.

4. Let your child put some of the leaves in the basket.

5. Enjoy jumping in the pile and throwing the leaves from the basket in the air to create a leaf storm.

Using the Leaves

- Use the leaves to make the outline of a square. The square might become an outdoor playhouse. Inside the square, pile leaves for the bed or sofa.

- Write your child's name with leaves on the cleared area.

- As a last resort, bag the leaves to be taken by the garbage man.

Note: This activity is not designed to get rid of the leaves in your yard, although it may. It is designed to use the leaves for playing and learning.

Dig It Up! Fill It In!

Digging is an adventure. Imagine what you might find!

What You Need

- shovels
- place to dig

What You Do

1. Choose a place to dig. Make sure that the sand or dirt in your first location is soft enough to ensure initial success.

2. Dig!
   At first, there is no need for a plan or a strategy. Your child will simply enjoy the accomplishment of digging a hole and filling it in. As you repeat the experience, you may want to identify what you are digging.

3. Add water to the experience and make a lake. Soon you will be creating and digging interconnecting systems of waterways.

> Keep a careful eye on your diggers. Three-year-old Mark and his cousin Jeff used their toy dump trucks and miniature shovels to fill in 20 holes that a workman had dug for our new deck. The play looked innocent enough from my vantage point in the garden, but when I had to pay to have the holes redrilled, I decided we needed a sandbox for digging.

Vehicle Wash

Set up a station for washing vehicles.

What You Need

- hose
- bucket
- big sponge
- some vehicles—toys, trikes and bikes, or your car!
- a nozzle that has a squeeze off-and-on handle
- markers and cardboard for a sign

What You Do

1. Set up the washing station.
   - Make a sign—*Tommy's Wash and Shine*
   - Coil the hose with nozzle attached.
   - Set out the bucket and sponge.

2. Start washing.

The same kind of washing station is a great way to clean toys and play dishes.

Bedtime

I'm all tired out,
But I'd rather play.
I don't want to sleep.
Why can't it be day?
Can you sing me a song?
Can you read me a tale?
Can you bring me a snack?
My bed is a jail!

Play and Learn to

- increase phonemic awareness
- develop memory and vocabulary
- improve ability to concentrate
- listen, remember, and retell
- learn about rhythm
- follow simple directions
- feel loved and safe

Activities

Fingerplays

Chant and sing simple rhyming verses as you do hand and finger actions.

What You Need

• a rhyme in your head (see page 52)

What You Do

1. When you first introduce a fingerplay, do it for your child several times. Sit on the bed facing your child and enjoy the fun. If your child does not automatically imitate your actions, suggest it.

2. Learn the fingerplays on the next three pages, one at a time. Then establish a bedtime fingerplay routine as you repeat all three each night. Substitute a new rhyme when you find one that's fun.

Three Fingerplays for Three-Year-Olds
Five Little Monkeys

Change the number of fingers for each verse

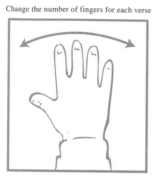

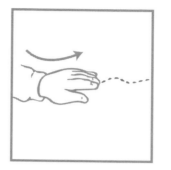

Five little monkeys
Sitting in the tree
Teasing Mr. Alligator,
"Can't catch me!"

Along came Mr. Alligator
Hungry as can be.

Snap!

Four little monkeys
Sitting in the tree
Teasing Mr. Alligator,
"Can't catch me!"
Along came Mr. Alligator
Hungry as can be.
Snap!

Three little monkeys
Sitting in the tree
Teasing Mr. Alligator,
"Can't catch me!"
Along came Mr. Alligator
Hungry as can be.
Snap!

Two little monkeys
Sitting in the tree
Teasing Mr. Alligator,
"Can't catch me!"
Along came Mr. Alligator
Hungry as can be.
Snap!

One little monkey
Sitting in the tree
Teasing Mr. Alligator,
"Can't catch me!"
Along came Mr. Alligator
Hungry as can be.
Snap!

No little monkeys
Sitting in the tree
There goes Mr. Alligator
Full as he can be!

Play and Learn with Your Three-Year-Old • EMC 4502

Where Is Thumbkin?

Where is Thumbkin?
Where is Thumbkin?

Here I am. Here I am.

How are you tonight, sir?
Very well, I thank you.

Run away.
Run away.

(Repeat with Pointer, Tall Man, Ring Man, and Pinky.)

Tall Man

Ring Man

Pointer

Pinky

Thumbkin

Ten Little Fingers

I have ten little fingers,
And they all belong to me.
I can make them do things.
Would you like to see?

I can shut them up tight
Or open them wide.

I can put them together
Or make them all hide.

I can make them jump high
Or make them go low.

I can fold them up quietly
And sit down just so.

Putting Teddy to Bed

Develop a routine for putting a favorite stuffed animal to bed for the night. Then follow the same routine with your child.

What You Need

- favorite stuffed animal
- bed for the animal (You could make one from a shoebox and an old blanket.)

What You Do

Note: Use the name of your child's special stuffed animal instead of "Teddy."

1. When it's bedtime, suggest that your child get Teddy ready for bed.
2. Take Teddy into the bathroom for washing and brushing.
3. Change Teddy into his pjs.
4. Read Teddy a story.
5. Tuck Teddy in.
6. Sing a lullaby.
7. Turn out the lights.

Tell a Story

**Occasionally tell your child a story instead of reading.
Later, encourage your child to tell you a story.**

What You Need

• a story in your head

What You Do

1. Tuck your child in bed or snuggle together in a chair for the story.

2. Tell the story.
   • Tell a true story about your child.
      Once upon a time there was a little girl named Chelsea. She loved to dress up in her mother's clothes. One day…
   • Tell a story to explain something that happened during the day.
      Once upon a time there was a cat named Herbie. Herbie lived with Jill and her dog Sandy. Herbie watched Jill throw the ball to Sandy. He watched as Sandy brought the ball back to Jill. Herbie was a smart cat. When Jill threw a wad of tissue paper on the floor, Herbie picked the wad up in his mouth and carried it over to Jill. What a good kitty!

3. After a while, encourage your child to become the storyteller.

Keep the stories short. Develop characters that are repeated in subsequent stories. (Herbie, my daughter's cat, showed up night after night in our stories.)

A Bedtime Comparison

Turn the lights off and on to compare what you see when it's light and when it's dark.

What You Need

• a light switch

What You Do

1. Have your child turn out the lights and wait for a few moments. Then ask,
   What can you see in the dark?

2. Talk about the things that you see.

3. Have your child turn the lights back on. Talk about how things look different when it is light.

4. Another time, look out the window and ask,
   What do you see outside when it's dark?

While-You-Wait Time

I can sit quietly
I know that I can.
I'll surprise you with
My attention span!

Play and Learn to

- identify the shapes of things
- practice counting
- sharpen memory and coordination
- develop vocabulary
- learn about qualities and characteristics
- practice patterning

Activities

Go on a Shape Hunt

Name all the things around you that are a specific shape.

What You Need

• the things around you

What You Do

1. Think of a shape and name it.
   a square

2. Look around. Help your child name all the things that are that shape.
   the window, the book, the table, the sign

3. Change shapes and repeat.

If your child is ready, introduce the concept of corners.

You're right, the table is a square.
Do you see this pointy edge?
We call this point a corner.
Let's count the corners on the table.

Can you find another square?
How many corners does that square have?

Just Count!

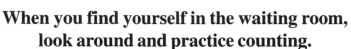

When you find yourself in the waiting room, look around and practice counting.

What You Need

- the waiting room

What You Do

Count together in different ways.

1. Count fingers.
   First, count just your child's fingers. Then add yours as well. Count together touching each finger as you count it. Then listen as your child counts. Help if you need to.

2. Count pockets.
   Find all the pockets in your child's clothes. Count them. Add your pockets as well.

3. Count pennies.
   Count the pennies in your coin purse. Make piles of ten pennies. Ask,
   Can you make three piles of ten?
   Try other coins.

4. Count chairs.
   Count the chairs in the room.
   Count the people in the room.
   Are there more chairs or more people?

Giraffe

**Waiting in a quiet place may be difficult.
Try playing *Giraffe*.**

What You Need

• a quiet place

What You Do

1. Explain to your child that a giraffe doesn't talk.
   Very often, it stands quietly and looks around.

2. Hold your child up high (like the tall giraffe)
   and ask,
   Can you be like a giraffe?

3. Your child is quiet and looks around.

As improbable as it sounds, this is a great game.
My children loved to play *Giraffe*. They would
have contests to see who could not talk for the
longest time.

What If?

Encourage your child to think creatively.

What You Need

• time together

What You Do

1. Propose a change. Ask,
    What if you had four feet?
    What if the sky was always purple?
    What if cars used tomato juice instead of gasoline?

2. Talk with your child about the effect of the change.

3. Let your child propose a *What if…*

My Notebook

For creating while waiting, carry a small notebook with pencil.

What You Need

- a small notebook—a memo-sized spiral one is great
- a pencil
- a piece of string

What You Do

1. Attach the pencil to the notebook.

2. Keep the notebook in your purse or pocket so that it is always handy.

3. Draw several lines on the page and ask your child to make something out of the lines.

4. Take turns drawing lines and creating things.

I framed a charming underwater scene that my 3-year-old nephew drew as we waited for a table at a restaurant. The seascape still hangs in my family room and Doug enjoys seeing his special creation whenever he visits.

Pattern and Eat

Carry a plastic container of small snacks for patterning fun.

What You Need

- small plastic container with lid
- little "nibbles" such as Cheerios®, raisins, grapes, marshmallows
- piece of paper

What You Do

1. Put a piece of paper on a solid surface.

2. Put a line of 4–6 "nibbles" in a line at the top of the paper.
   grape • grape • marshmallow • grape • grape

3. Have your child duplicate the line.

4. Eat the pattern.

5. Make more complicated patterns.

Travel Time

Here's what I know
Most things can go!
Wagons, Trains,
Taxis, Planes,
Tractors, Trikes,
Rockets, Bikes,
A water ski,
Kiddie car, and me.

Play and Learn to

- develop fine-motor coordination

- improve memory and coordination

- identify colors

- recite rhymes

- learn about rhythm

- increase phonemic awareness

Activities

Stringing Cheerios®

A bag of Cheerios® and a pipe cleaner are easy carry-alongs for developing dexterity.

What You Need

• self-closing plastic bag or small container with a lid

• some Cheerios®

• large pipe cleaner

What You Do

1. Give your child a large pipe cleaner with one end folded over and the bag of Cheerios®.

2. Have your child string the Cheerios® on the pipe cleaner.

3. Begin by simply stringing the Cheerios®. Later designate a number to be strung.
   Can you put five Cheerios® on the pipe cleaner?

Play and Learn with Your Three-Year-Old • EMC 4502

Sing a Song

Singing together is a great way to develop an awareness of the sounds of language.

What You Need

• songs in your head (Try the ones on the following pages.)

• a tape player and tapes (optional)—You can sing along and you don't have to remember the words!

What You Do

Sing!

The old favorites you remember from your childhood will be fine or you can learn a few new tunes. Don't worry about getting the words or the tune perfect. Just enjoy. Start with nursery rhymes and move on to those wonderful multiverse tales that go on forever, such as *The Wheels on the Bus* or *Down on Grandpa's Farm*. If you don't know the tune, chant the words or make up a tune of your own.

After your child becomes familiar with the words, stop singing just before the final word so he or she can finish the line.

The wheels on the bus
Go round and round
Go round and roun

Songs to sing with a three-year-old

The Wheels on the Bus

The wheels on the bus
Go round and round,
Round and round,
Round and round.
The wheels on the bus
Go round and round
All over the town!

The driver on the bus
Says "Move on back!
Move on back!
Move on back!"
The driver on the bus
Says "Move on back!"
All over the town!

Repeat, using the following verses:
The people on the bus
Go up and down.

The babies on the bus
Go "Wah! Wah! Wah!"

The mothers on the bus
Go "Shh, shh, shh."

The wipers on the bus
Go swish, swish, swish.

The doors on the bus
Open and close.

Make up some more verses as you sing!

Down on Grandpa's Farm

Down on Grandpa's farm there is a big pink pig.
Down on Grandpa's farm there is a big pink pig.
The pig, it makes a noise like this:
   SNORT!
The pig, it makes a noise like this:
   SNORT!

Oh, we're on the way.
Oh, we're on the way.
On the way to Grandpa's farm.

Down on Grandpa's farm there is an old white horse.
Down on Grandpa's farm there is an old white horse.
The horse, it makes a noise like this:
   WHINNY!
The horse, it makes a noise like this:
   WHINNY!

Oh, we're on the way.
Oh, we're on the way.
On the way to Grandpa's farm.

Think of other animals that you might see on a farm and add them to your song.

If You're Happy and You Know It

If you're happy and you know it,
Clap your hands.
If you're happy and you know it,
Clap your hands.
If you're happy and you know it,
And you're not afraid to show it,
If you're happy and you know it,
Clap your hands.

Try—Stamp your feet.
    Nod your head.
    Turn around.
    Shout hurray!

Then, change the feeling.
    If you're shy and you know it,
    Hide your eyes.

    If you're tired and you know it,
    Give a yawn.

    If you're angry and you know it,
    Stamp your foot.

Mystery Bag

Capitalize on your three-year-old's love of surprises with a mystery bag.

What You Need

- small pillowcase or other cloth bag
- yard of ribbon or yarn
- several familiar toys
- a new toy (optional)

What You Need

1. Put one toy in the pillowcase and tie it shut with the ribbon.
2. Have your child feel the hidden item and try to guess what it is.
3. Open the bag and discover what's inside.
4. Change toys.
5. End with the new toy.

Story Time

Read me a story.
Let's try this good one.
We've read it before—
A good book rerun.

Play and Learn to

- tell and retell stories

- predict what will happen next

- identify objects in illustrations and photographs

- act out stories

- make and use puppets

- start from the front of a book and turn pages

- understand that a word stands for the name of a thing

Activities

Shared Reading

Sit with your child on your lap or snuggle together and share a favorite book. Continue to develop the good reading practices that you began when your child was one and two. Reading is ageless.

One of the joys of sharing books and stories with young children is watching their reactions to the same book change as they grow and mature. The simple text and bold drawings in *Brown Bear, Brown Bear* by Bill Martin, Jr. is a favorite among young listeners.

- At first, three-year-olds will enjoy the rhythm of the words. They will say the names of the animals as they appear on the pages and imitate the sounds that the animals make.

- Soon they'll start turning the pages and calling out the animal on the next page before they've even seen it.

- Before long they will be reciting the text word for word.

What You Need

Good books!
- Books about children
- Books about seasons and nature
- Books about animals
- Alphabet books
- Simple riddle and guessing books

What You Do

1. Preview the book as you begin. Turn the pages and point out the objects in the illustrations. Relate the objects to your child's experiences. Use your child's name.
   Look at the bear.
   Is it Josh's teddy?
   Talk about your child's favorite activities.
   See the little girl in the book.
   She's taking a bath.
   You just took a bath, too.

2. Read the text with feeling.

> Choose books with repetition and pattern in the words and story structure.

A few suggestions:

Bookstores and libraries are filled with wonderful books for you and your child to share. There are a number of excellent read-aloud guides that will help you choose good literature appropriate to the age of your child.

Buy a few special books to enjoy over and over again at bedtime. Be sure to consider these books, just a few of my favorites:

Barnyard Banter by Denise Fleming; Owlet, 1997.
Berenstain's B Book by Stan and Jan Berenstain; Random House, 1997.
Color Surprises by Chuck Murphy; Little Simon, 1997.
Color Zoo by Lois Ehlert; Harpercollins, 1997.
Dr. Seuss's ABC: An Amazing Book by Dr. Seuss; Random House, 1996.
Exactly the Opposite by Tana Hoban; Mulberry Books, 1997.
From Head to Toe by Eric Carle; Harpercollins, 1997.
Lunch by Denise Fleming; Henry Holt, 1998.
Mouse Paint by Ellen Stoll Walsh; Red Wagon, 1995.
Richard Scarry's Best Word Book Ever by Richard Scarry; Golden Press, 1980.

Practice important prereading skills as you read.

A Note about Reading

The most important thing you can do for your child is **read**. Three-year-olds still enjoy books about everyday life, but they also enjoy hearing about animals and different forms of transportation. They love to hear the same story over and over again. Many three-year-olds enjoy looking at books by themselves. Enjoy the freedom of reading beside your child as well as to your child.

1. Retelling

    Your child's ability to retell, to summarize, and to correctly order the events in a story are indicators of reading readiness. When you have finished reading a story, ask your child to tell what the story was about.

        Tell me about what happened in the story.

2. Predicting

    Stop reading and ask your child to predict what will happen next. Listen carefully and then read on to see if the prediction was correct.

3. Identifying Pictures

    Point to a picture. Say,

        Tell me what this is.

         or

        Show me a _____.

    And have your child point to an object.

Honeybee, busy little bee. All day long you're making honey while...

A Flap Book

Create a flap-board book for your child to read and enjoy.

What You Need

- posterboard pages (Choose the size that you want the book to be and make all the pages the same size. Three-year-olds love little books, so you may want to make the pages small.)

- index cards

- photos or illustrations

- hole punch

- scissors

- glue

- metal ring or string

What You Do

1. Glue a photo to the posterboard page.

2. Label the photo with a single word or simple sentence.

3. Position the index card over the top of the photo to form a flap.

4. Glue the top edge of the index card to hold it in place.

5. Write a question on the index card.

6. Punch holes in the top left-hand corner of all the pages.

7. Fasten the pages together with a metal ring or a piece of string.

8. Read and enjoy the book.

> Vary the questions on the cards.
> *Where's Tori? (sleeping, eating, digging, walking)*
> *What's inside?*

story time • story time • story time • story time • story time • story time • story time • story time • story time • story time • story time • story time

Act It Out

Enjoy dramatic play as you retell your favorite nursery rhymes.

What You Need

• a nursery rhyme

What You Do

1. Assign parts.

2. Sometimes you will need to establish the setting.
   Let's use this stool as the tuffet.

3. You repeat the rhyme.
   Little Miss Muffet

   The child moves through the actions.
   Sat on her tuffet.

   Stop for key lines.
   Sat down beside her… (scream)

4. Continue to end of the rhyme.

5. Take your bows.

6. Suggest that your child do the narration.

Puppets

Three-year-olds love puppets. Use them to tell stories, to make up new stories, or to just talk.

What You Need

- puppets
(You can buy ready-made ones or make your own. See page 79.)

What You Do

1. Put a puppet on your hand.

2. Give one to your child.

3. Start talking as the puppet.
   - try telling a familiar story
   - try a familiar situation like going to bed
   - try out a new situation like visiting Grandma alone

Puppet Directions

Mitten Puppet
Materials:
- single mitten
- felt
- glue or needle and thread
- marker

1. Add ears, eyes, mouth, and other details to mitten. Either draw them on or cut them out of felt and glue or sew them on.

2. Put on the mitten and use the puppet!

Pants-Leg Puppet
Materials:
- leg cut off an old pair of pants
- yarn
- stuffing (shredded plastic bags)
- pencil

1. Cut a piece about 12 inches long from the leg of an old pair of pants.

2. Turn the piece inside out. Gather and tie one end shut.

3. Turn the piece right-side out. Stuff the closed end to form the head. Tie off neck.

4. Cut arm holes for puppeteer's fingers.

5. Decorate puppet as desired.

6. Insert a dowel into puppet's head. Hold the puppet as shown. Thumb and forefinger are arms.

Look At Me— A Special Book

Create a special collection of your child's drawings, stories, and photographs.

What You Need

- a computer or traditional writing tools
- paper
- photos or child-drawn illustrations
- a scrapbook

What You Do

1. With your child, choose photos or pictures to put in the book.
2. Ask your child to tell about the picture. Record what he or she says as a caption for the picture.
3. Put the pictures into the scrapbook.
4. Read it often.

Add stories that your child tells you and stories about things that your child does. Note the date of every entry and any other interesting circumstances. The scrapbook will become a prized possession.

This is my ted
He has a crow
and I love him.